HE

Herald of Hope

Reflections on the Life and Spirit of
Saint Charles of Mount Argus

OVADA

2007

Published in the United Kingdom by

OVADA BOOKS

Saint Mungo's Retreat, 52 Parson Street
Glasgow G4 0RX

Tel/Fax +44 (0)141 552 5523

ISBN 978-1-905965-01-4

www.ovadabooks.com
info@ovadabooks.com

Cum permissu superiorum

A Catalogue record for this book is available from the British Library

Printed in Glasgow by Bell & Bain Ltd
www.bell-bain.co.uk
∞

Contents

Introduction v

List of Contributors vii

I. A Saintly Life PAUL FRANCIS SPENCER CP 1

II. Uplifted in Prayer PAUL FRANCIS SPENCER CP 7

III. The Presence of God PAUL FRANCIS SPENCER CP 17

IV. A Mystery of Suffering AIDAN TROY CP 23

V. Doing God's Will BRIAN D'ARCY CP 29

VI. The Passion-Pattern in Life IGNATIUS WATERS CP 39

VII. A Healing Blessing FRANK KEEVINS CP 45

VIII. The Stranger Among Us MARTIN COFFEY CP 49

IX. A Mother's Love MARTIN COFFEY CP 59

Introduction

What can someone who died over a hundred years ago possibly say to us today? Saint Charles of Mount Argus died in Dublin in 1893. Can his life speak to people who live in a very different world? These reflections try to answer that question.

Originally given as homilies at the 2006 Novena of Hope in the Church of Saint Paul of the Cross, Mount Argus, Dublin, these nine meditations on Charles' life and spirit attempt to allow him to dialogue with us, to share with us his sense of what it means to be a disciple of Jesus Christ. The tone of the various texts is somewhat conversational, and the variety of writers provides a complimentarity of perspectives, as each chooses elements of Charles' character and incidents from his life to illustrate different facets of his message.

The saints, the liturgy tells us, are 'the living Gospel for all to hear'. In the different periods of history, they make the Gospel not just heard but also seen. Saint Charles' impact on the people of his time was more visible than audible or even legible. Above all, his was a vocation of presence, not easy to express in words. The authors of these reflections have been touched by his presence and now seek to communicate it to others. May their efforts succeed in bringing Charles' spirit to life for all who will read this book.

List of Contributors

Martin Coffey CP is Provincial of Saint Patrick's Province of the Congregation of the Passion. Having taught philosophy for several years in Africa, he returned to Ireland in 2000. He is also President of the Conference of Religious of Ireland (CORI).

Brian D'Arcy CP is a well-known writer and broadcaster. Rector of Mount Argus at the time of Saint Charles' beatification, he is the author of *Saint Charles of Mount Argus*, a biography of Charles which has sold over 100,000 copies.

Frank Keevins CP worked in religious and spiritual formation for many years. He is currently Rector of Mount Argus.

Paul Francis Spencer CP is the author of *To Heal the Broken Hearted*, which is considered the most complete account of Charles' life available in English. It has also been published in Dutch.

Aidan Troy CP, a former General Consultor of the Passionists and currently Rector of Holy Cross, Ardoyne, Belfast, is the author of *Holy Cross: A Personal Experience.*

Ignatius Waters CP was Provincial of Saint Patrick's Province when Saint Charles was beatified in 1988. Since then, he has been engaged in preaching and parish work in Ireland and in South Africa.

I

A Saintly Life

PAUL FRANCIS SPENCER CP

Saint Charles of Mount Argus was born in Munstergeleen, in the Netherlands, on 11 December 1821. When he was twenty-five years old, he joined the Passionists. Two years after his ordination, he was sent to England where he worked for five years, after which he moved to Ireland, arriving at Saint Paul's Retreat, Mount Argus on 9 July 1857. Apart from a stay of a few years in England, he spent the remainder of his life at Mount Argus, where he died on 5 January, 1893. This is an outline of his life with dates, but it doesn't tell you anything about the person.

What kind of person was Father Charles? Well, first of all, I can tell you what he was not. He was not a great scholar. Nor was he a great theologian. When he was a boy in his village at home, the people in the village said he knew only two roads — the road to the church, and the road to the school. He knew the road to the school so well because he spent so many years going to it, and making very little progress. Indeed, it was only after his military service that he returned home, having decided that he wanted to be a Passionist priest, that things began to improve. When he went back to school after being in the army, he began at last to make some progress in his studies. But he was not Saint Thomas Aquinas. We don't remember him because of his theological writings.

He was not a great preacher, either. In the first place, he didn't speak very good English, and people who came to Mount Argus said that it was often very difficult to understand what he was saying. This was a common problem in the early days in Mount Argus, because a number of the first Passionists who went there were Dutch or Belgian or Italian. Even Blessed Dominic Barberi, the Italian who gave the first Passionist mission in Dublin, in Saint Audeon's Church in High Street, was not much better when it came to speaking English. On one occasion, when Blessed Dominic was giving a retreat to nuns, he intended to quote the Bible and to say to the sisters, 'Without faith, you cannot be saved', but instead he said, 'My dear sisters, without face, you cannot be shaved'! This is true too, of course, but it was not what he was trying to say. Father Charles sometimes made similar mistakes.

Although he was neither a scholar nor a preacher, the people of Dublin saw two things in him which drew them to him. The first was his love for God: his love for Jesus Christ, and especially Jesus in his suffering, in his Passion. The other thing the people of Dublin saw in Father Charles was his love for people – especially for the sick, the suffering, those in difficulty or in need. And that is the secret of Father Charles.

What kind of person was he? What was he like? There are two pictures of Father Charles with which we are familiar. The first is one which was traditionally used on prayer leaflets; it is a black and white photograph taken not long before he died. It is said that the whole community was assembled for this picture so that Father Charles was not to know that it was really a picture of him alone. In the photograph, we can see others standing behind him, while he appears quite unconscious of the photographer. Looking at it, we see an old man who is sitting and holding something in his hand. He is holding a book with a crucifix on top of the book, and he is staring at it: his eyes and his mind are fixed completely on the crucifix. The other picture that we know well is the banner which was hanging outside Saint Peter's Basilica in Rome on 16 October 1988, the day Charles was beatified. In that picture, we see Saint Charles standing outside the Church of Saint Paul of the Cross at Mount Argus, surrounded by a crowd of people: sick and healthy, young and old, rich and poor. The figure in this picture looks straight ahead. He is full of energy; he has a commanding presence. This is someone who draws you to him by looking straight at you. When we look at these two pictures, we might at first sight think that these are two different people: the one with his eyes down, looking at the cross, and the other surrounded by people and looking straight at us. But the truth is that for Father Charles, just as for ourselves, there was more than one dimension to his life.

What kind of person was he? Charles was a shy person. Those who knew him tell us that. He was shy; he was a little bit timid, a little bit nervous; he could suffer from anxiety at times. We don't think of saints as suffering from things like that, but he did. He was scrupulous sometimes; and he was a bit awkward in company. He wasn't the kind of person who goes into a room and suddenly takes over, with everyone having to listen to them. He was a person who in normal circumstances would have walked into the room and nobody would have noticed. But he was somebody who, although shy, loved being with people. He loved company and he loved meeting people. He loved listening to people and being with them. In his heart, there was a great compassion for people in any kind of need, especially those who were sick.

There's a piece of paper in Mount Argus, on the back of which Saint Charles had written some notes for himself, including a number of resolutions that he wanted to keep. Perhaps some other Passionist had 'corrected' him, as his superiors (and others) used to do, so he wrote down what he should be doing. When we read these resolutions, we see him saying, more or less: 'I must stop spending so much time with people; I should be thinking more about the Lord. I should be looking at the crucifix. I should be praying more. And when people come to the door to be blessed, or when I go to the church to bless the sick, I should just go down and give them the blessing with the relic, say a little word and then go back to the monastery, instead of spending so much time with them'. And he says, 'I should learn from the good example of Father George, because that's what he does.'

More than a hundred years later, I'm sorry to say that before reading those words I had never heard of Father George. I have no idea who he was; and here was Saint Charles of Mount Argus saying, 'I really should be more like Father George'. Now, isn't there a lesson in that for all of us?

Charles was a man whose love for God and love for people was clear to everyone he met. When the canonisation process (or enquiry) was opened in the 1930's, a number of people who had known him, both members of the Passionist community and people to whom Charles ministered, were interviewed by the Diocesan Tribunal. One of them said an extraordinary, yet very simple, thing: 'When you talked to Father Charles, you had the impression you were speaking to someone who was an intimate friend of God'. That is how he summed up Saint Charles of Mount Argus.

In Saint John's Gospel, Jesus says, 'I do not call you servants any more. I call you friends.' Charles was someone who learned what that means. The secret of Father Charles — his love for God, his love for people — came from the truth that he was an intimate friend of God. We are invited by Jesus to follow Charles' example: to become God's friends, to live in friendship with God, to have Jesus as our companion each day of our life, and to learn from Jesus love for God and love for those around us. Father Charles can teach us how, through loving God in prayer and loving our brothers and sisters in their need, we can become in truth the friends of God.

II

Uplifted in Prayer

PAUL FRANCIS SPENCER CP

During his years at Mount Argus, Saint Charles rarely celebrated Mass at the High Altar. Father Salvian, who was a member of the community at that time and who kept a diary, tells us that the rector only assigned Charles to a public Mass at the High Altar when there was nobody else available. Otherwise, Charles normally said Mass somewhere else. As it happens, the place where he normally said Mass is one of the few altars in the church which date from the time of Father Charles; most of the other altars are newer. Father Charles normally said his daily Mass at what we called the Magdalene altar, the altar of Saint Mary Magdalene, just beside the monastery door, near the entrance to the church. The reason he said Mass there, and the reason he wasn't put down to say the public Masses, was because he took too long.

The Mass offered by Saint Charles normally lasted about an hour. In those days the Mass was in Latin. During the week, there was no homily. Even on Sundays, there was only one reading before the Gospel. I remember, as an altar boy in the days when the Mass was said in Latin, that a usual weekday Mass lasted about twenty minutes. But Father Charles' Mass, we are told, normally took at least an hour, and sometimes longer.

The altar servers, of course, did not like being put down for Father Charles' Mass, because it meant they were going to have to wait longer to get home for breakfast. Why was his Mass so long? It was not that he was distracted, nor was he becoming scrupulous and repeating things. But at times, in the course of the celebration of Mass, he would be so caught up in prayer that he would lose awareness of his surroundings. One of the witnesses, a former altar server who was called to the enquiry for his cause of canonisation, says that when this happened, the server would tug at his vestments, pulling the alb to try to bring him out of this prayerful state. If that didn't work, they would go and find Father Salvian, who would come and stand beside Father Charles at the altar and put a stole on; this usually would bring Charles back to his senses and he would continue the Mass, though sometimes, after a few minutes, it would happen again.

Another unusual thing which would happen during Charles' Mass had to do with little bits of paper. When he would be saying Mass at the Magdalene altar, he would take all these bits of paper out of his pocket and put them on the altar in front of him. And what were these bits of paper? Well, there were letters he had received from people asking for prayers, or little notes people had handed him requesting that he would remember someone at Mass, or names he had written down of people he had promised to pray for. And when he came to the part of the Mass where we remember those for whom we promised to pray ('Remember, Lord, Your people, especially those for whom we now pray'), he would stop what he was doing and go through all his bits of paper: all the letters and notes and little petitions that people had given him.

The community thought he was quite eccentric; nobody else did that. The prayer intentions for the community at Mount Argus were, and are, written up in the sacristy and outside the community chapel ('the choir'). But Father Charles had dozens of bits of paper, and he would look at all these so that everyone who had asked for his prayers would be remembered. How very odd, the others thought.

Be honest and think of how many times somebody has said to you: 'Oh, will you pray for a special intention, will you pray for this person who is sick, will you remember this person who is having an operation, will you pray for my son or daughter who is having an exam (or going for an interview for a job)?', and you say, 'Oh yes, I'll pray for them'. And then a week later you remember, and you say to yourself, 'Oh, I meant to pray for that person and I forgot.' Maybe you say to yourself, 'Well, it was included because I say when I pray: for all of those people for whom I promised to pray'. You have a kind of a blanket that covers all these people that you spoke to in the street or who spoke to you at the church door on your way out of Mass, to whom you said 'Oh, yes, I'll pray', and then forgot.

But for Father Charles, it was a sacred duty to pray for all those who asked for his intercession. This was a distinctive mark of his life. Why did he do this very eccentric thing, emptying his pockets when he said Mass, putting all those bits of paper on top of the altar? Because Father

Charles believed in the power of prayer. He believed that praying for someone does make a difference. Sometimes when we pray, maybe for someone who is seriously ill, at the back of our minds we say to ourselves, 'Is this really going to do anything? Will my prayer really make a difference here?' Father Charles believed in the power of prayer. He believed in the words spoken by Jesus in the Gospel: 'Anything you ask for in my name, believe that it is yours, and it will be granted to you' – Ask, believe, receive.

Saint Charles took those words of Jesus to heart. He prayed for all those who asked for prayers because he believed in the power of prayer. He believed in the power of God, and in the promises of Jesus. Remember how, in another part of the Gospel, Jesus says, 'Ask and you will receive'; before that he says, 'If you who are evil know how to give good things to those you love, how much more will your heavenly Father give you what you need when you ask him'.

It wasn't that Father Charles believed in the power of his own prayers over everyone else's; it wasn't all about him: 'I'll pray for you and when I pray for you, it will happen, because my prayers are special. My prayers are better than his prayers'. It wasn't like that. In the canonisation processes, one of the people interviewed was Father Malachy Gavin, who was a Passionist student at Mount Argus in the time of Father Charles. When he was called as a witness to the tribunal for the cause of canonisation, in the 1930s, he told a very interesting story. One morning in the monastery, he came down for breakfast and found Father Charles there. Father Charles was standing stirring his coffee, saying nothing. Malachy, the young Passionist full of wit and self-confidence and maybe a little skepticism, said, 'Well, Father Charles, any miracles today?' and Father Charles, he tells us, didn't even look up. He just kept on stirring his coffee, and then he said, 'Dear Malachy, the same God who created you created me'. Father Charles believed in the power of God, not in the power of Father Charles.

When he prayed, he prayed with faith, believing that God listens to our prayers: 'Ask and you shall receive'. When we pray, we open our hearts to the grace of God and when we pray, things that seemed impossible become possible. When we pray our life is changed.

More than twenty-five years ago, I met a man who told me that his grandfather had once gone to Mount Argus to be blessed by Father Charles. When his grandfather was still a relatively young man, he had been diagnosed as having cancer in an advanced state, and had been told that he had only about a month to live. His family suggested to him that he should go to Mount Argus and be blessed by Father Charles.

He went to the monastery and asked to see Father Charles. Father Charles came down to the parlour and listened to his story. He prayed with the sick man and blessed him. After he had finished praying and blessing him, he said to him, 'You are not going to recover from this and, in about a month's time, you will die. So now you have to prepare yourself; prepare yourself to pass from this life to the next'. The grandson told me that his grandfather went home and was perfectly at peace; there was a joy and a radiance about him which everyone could see. Those last weeks of his life became precious to him, and to his wife and family. He spent his last days surrounded by the love of his family, supported by his wife and family, and supporting them by his love. He died a peaceful and a holy death.

The man who told me this story said to me that his family always believed that they had received a miracle through the intercession of Father Charles; but it was not a miracle of physical healing. It was not the miracle for which his grandfather had gone to Mount Argus. The miracle that he had gone looking for was that he would be cured, that the sickness would leave him, and that he would live a long and healthy life; but the miracle he received was a different one; because the miracle he received was peace. The miracle he received was the grace of God, the grace of a happy death. He received a different kind of healing, not a healing of the body but a healing of the spirit.

When we pray, sometimes we expect the answer to come in a certain way. But that family learned by experience that the answer to their prayer did not come in the way that they expected, and yet the answer they received was just as rich as, or even richer than, what they had been hoping for.

When we pray, we open ourselves up to the grace of God. When we pray, we hold our hands out to God. We pray with open hands; we invite God to do something; and God who sees our heart, who knows our life, who knows us better than we know ourselves, reaches into our heart to give us what is best: 'How much more will your Heavenly Father give you what you need when you ask him'.

There are times when we are praying and we don't know what we need, and so our prayer has to be a handing over of our life to God. Here we try to allow God to be God in our lives, to allow God to be the one who decides, the one who shapes our life, the one who calls us closer to himself. We do this because, in the life of prayer, there is always the invitation from God to a deeper relationship with him. At the heart of all prayer is the relationship with God in Jesus Christ. There is nothing wrong with asking God for things. Jesus tells us to ask when we pray, and to ask with faith, to pray with confidence for what we need. But we need to remember that, when we do open our hearts and our lives to God, he will draw us beyond ourselves. There is always an element of risk in praying, because you do not know where it is going to lead. Sometimes we can even be afraid to pray for certain things in case our prayers are answered. That element of risk is always there, because God may just answer our prayer in a way that we did not expect, and maybe even in a way that we did not want. But Jesus says, 'Ask and you shall receive, seek and you shall find, knock and the door shall be opened to you'. When you knock, and he opens the door, he invites you to walk in: not to walk into a confined space, but into a bigger world which is the world of God's grace.

When we look at our life, we think we know what is best for us. (We usually think we know what is best for everyone else as well.) We know what is best for us, we know what we want, we know when we want it, we know how it's going to happen; but when we let God enter our life, he invites us out of that little homemade space of ours into a bigger world. And that is a risky business.

At the heart of all of this, what is it that God is offering us? In Saint John's Gospel, Jesus goes to the well in Samaria, at a place called Sichar. He sits down at the well in the middle of the day; a woman comes out to draw water, and she gets into conversation with Jesus. He says to her, 'If you knew the gift of God, and the one to whom you are speaking, you would have asked him and he would have given you living water'. If we can only recognise who it is we are talking to when we pray, and allow our eyes to be opened by faith, and allow our hearts and our desires to be expanded by grace, then prayer opens up our world. And at the heart of all this, what is the answer to prayer?

Think of all the things that we ask for, all the different things we seek when we pray, and remember that, ultimately, the bottom line is this: God has only one thing he wants to give us. We pray for lots of different things, but God has only one thing to give us, and the only thing God has to give us is himself. When we pray, when we spend time with God and open our heart to his grace, he offers to us the gift of himself. He offers to us that precious gift which is a relationship with him. In the Gospel, Jesus talks about a treasure hidden in the field, a pearl of great price. In our relationship with God, the pearl or treasure, the thing of infinite value is the gift of union with God. When we find it, we are content to let go of everything else so that we can have it, because in having it, we have everything; and the end of all our asking, the end of all our searching, is to be united with him.

He offers us a relationship more close and more real than any human relationship. In the Gospel, he says to us, 'Come to me, all you who labour and are burdened, and I will give you rest'. He gave that peace to a dying man through the blessing of Father Charles over a hundred years ago. He offers that same peace to us when we pray.

III

The Presence of God

PAUL FRANCIS SPENCER CP

Father Charles was somebody who lived his whole life in God's presence and in the awareness of that presence. I have already mentioned how people in the village where he grew up said that he only knew two roads, the road to the school and the road to the church, and if he was not in one place, he would be in the other place. When he was young, there would be evenings when he did not come home from school; it would be getting dark and one of his parents would go looking for him. They knew where to find him because he would be in the church. He would have stopped in the church on his way home from school and lost track of the time; he did not realise how long he had been there.

When he was still living at home, he joined a confraternity in the village parish; it was the Confraternity of the Blessed Sacrament. Part of the life of the members of that confraternity was to spend time each day in Eucharistic adoration. So it was that from an early age, before he became a Passionist religious, he was already accustomed to daily Eucharistic adoration, spending time each day in prayer in the presence of Jesus in the Blessed Sacrament. That spirit of prayer in God's presence was something that he tried to carry with him throughout the day.

As a Passionist, he would have tried, as all the early Passionists did, to put into practice the command of Jesus to pray always. When we read the lives of the early Passionists or the writings of the first followers of Saint Paul of the Cross, we see the preoccupation that they had with the words of Jesus in the Gospel: 'Pray at all times'. They tried to make those words of Jesus come alive through the practice of the presence of God, cultivating a continual awareness that they were truly in God's loving presence. We know that one of the ways that Father Charles did this was by carrying a little crucifix in his hand as he walked around the monastery or as he went from the monastery to the church. When he was walking from one place to another he always had in his hand the little crucifix, trying to focus not just his eyes but his mind and heart on the presence of Jesus.

One of Charles' contemporaries at Mount Argus, Father Salvian, tells us in his diary of an accident which happened because Father Charles was focusing on the crucifix. One day, there were plumbers working in the monastery, repairing some pipes. They had taken a cover off the pipe case, leaving a hole in the ground where all the pipes came together, and had gone for tea without replacing the cover. Father Charles came along with his little crucifix in his hand, with his eyes fixed on the crucifix and his mind focused on God, and he fell down the hole. Father Salvian had to go for help to pull Charles out of the hole and get him onto the floor again. So keeping your eyes always on the crucifix is not something that I recommend to you, especially in traffic, but you can keep your heart fixed on the Lord throughout the day which is what Charles himself was intent on doing.

Each day, after celebrating Mass at the Magdalene Altar, Saint Charles would return to the community chapel on the top floor of the monastery. He would return there to make his thanksgiving with the rest of the community: brothers, students and priests. Then he would go for his cup of coffee, after which he would come back up to the choir and go from there to a quiet, secluded corner of the monastery to spend another few hours in prayer. Going through the choir sacristy, there is a kind of a bridge, a passageway which links the bell tower to the monastery. This is where Charles would often go to pray in the morning after his cup of coffee, knowing that he would not be disturbed there and that nobody would see him. There he could be alone in the presence of God, kneeling on the cold stone floor for an hour or two until the time would come for him to go down to the church to bless the sick.

In the evening he would usually be found again in the choir, praying before the tabernacle in the presence of Jesus in the Blessed Sacrament, just as he had done as a schoolboy, a kind of a living sanctuary lamp before the presence of God. Father Eugene Nevin, who was a member of the community at that time, tells us in his *Recollections of Father Charles* that sometimes when Charles was praying there, the sanctuary lamp would go out; he would go looking for the student who was the choir sacristan and say, with an expression all his own, 'the lamp of the Lamb of God has gone out'. But that light was

burning in his own heart, that light of faith in the abiding presence of God. Father Charles carried that light of
God's presence throughout the day.

Those who knew him tell us that he always seemed to
be praying. Even at night when the cab would come to
bring him to the hospital or to a house where there was
a sick person, he would ask the cab driver for a candle
so that he could read from his book of prayers as he was
travelling from Mount Argus into the centre of Dublin. The cab drivers always had a candle ready for Father
Charles, because they knew that he prayed at all times
or at least he tried to pray at all times. Charles knew that
he was living always in God's presence and that he was
never alone.

In Saint Luke's Gospel, we read about two men making a journey from Jerusalem to a village called Emmaus.
Where they were going to didn't matter; what mattered
to them was that they wanted to get away from where
they were. They were followers of Jesus who had lived
through the events of Good Friday, through what to
them seemed the tragic events of the Crucifixion. All
they wanted to do now was to get away from all that, to
get away from Jerusalem. They set out on the road to Emmaus and Jesus himself, Jesus who is risen from the dead,
came and walked by their side. In the Gospel, Saint Luke
says that something prevented them from recognising
Jesus. In our own lives, Christ is always there, no matter
where we are, no matter what is happening and no matter how we feel. Jesus is always present in our life, but we
are not always aware of his presence. Sometimes this is
because we have a particular idea of what the presence
of God should be like. We can think that the presence of

God should mean that we avoid the pain of this life, but here we see Jesus walking with the two disciples and accompanying them in their pain.

When we live in the presence of God, it does not mean that our suffering is going to disappear; nor does it mean that we are going to have an easy life. But it means that we will never be alone. In the Gospel passage, what was it that prevented those two men from recognising Jesus? Perhaps it was the weight of discouragement, we might even say disillusionment, that was theirs at having lived through the events of Good Friday. They thought this Messiah would be a painless saviour, one who would suddenly just make everything fine so that there would be no more problems in the world. What does Jesus say to them? 'You foolish men, so slow to believe the full message of the prophets: was it not ordained that the Christ should suffer and so enter into his glory?' Jesus had to open their eyes to understand that their suffering was not an absence of God, but that in some mysterious way it was still part of God's presence. In other words, God is not just present in my life when the sun is shining; in the winter of my life, when it rains and gets cold, God is not absent. He promises to be with me every day of my life, through all the experiences of my life and in everything that happens to me.

Father Charles was someone who knew difficulty throughout his life. He struggled with his own limitations, with the pain of loneliness, being far from his family, with anxiety and with poor health. Yet, in all of this, he knew that Jesus was with him. When the two men in the Gospel story reach the place they are going to, they say to Jesus 'stay with us because it is nearly evening'. And he goes in and stays with them, and they recognise him 'in the breaking of the bread'. When darkness comes into our own life, in moments when everything is not bright and sunny and cheerful, in the dark night of our life, he is still there. We may not always feel that presence, but he is there. He promises to be with us especially in the Sacrament of the Eucharist, which was the very heart, the very centre, of Father Charles' spiritual life. In the Sacrament of his Body and Blood He has left us an abiding presence. And that presence of Jesus in the Eucharist doesn't depend on how we feel or what we believe. It depends on his promise and the power of the Sacrament.

Jesus wishes to be our companion on our journey through life. He wishes to come in and stay with us when the darkness is setting in. He does not want us to be alone; he wants us always to be in his presence. He asks us to be aware, to realise that he is there and that that we are not alone, to know that he is by our side with his mercy, with his grace and with his love.

IV

A Mystery of Suffering

AIDAN TROY CP

A young Jewish girl was about to leave home. She visited her Rabbi to ask for his blessing and advice about the future and her religious practice in her new surroundings. In the course of their conversation she put this question to her Rabbi: 'How do I know if a Rabbi is genuine?'

He replied that this was an interesting question. He suggested that she ask any Rabbi she would meet if he could explain suffering. If he can, you will know that he is not genuine.

I can't explain suffering to you either. Neither does Jesus find suffering easy – in the Garden of Gethsemane he cries out, 'My God, my God why have you forsaken me?'

You don't need me to tell you that suffering and death surround you and break your heart:

You think of the heartbreak

You think of the tears

You wonder where God is in all of what is happening

You feel so isolated

Look for a moment at Jesus on the Cross and know that there will never be a single and comprehensive answer to the meaning of suffering – whether it is physical, emotional, psychological or spiritual. Think of the demands made on Saint Charles when he arrived in Mount Argus on 9 July 1857. People thronged to see him as his reputation spread. We can hear the tone of desperation as people search for a cure for a loved one. One man demands, 'You must cure my son!' Charles' reply is clear, 'There is no must with God'.

We may wonder if we or our loved ones are suffering as a punishment for sin. Jesus rejects this when people ask him if a man born blind was suffering because of sin. The same connection was rejected by Jesus when talking about a tower that had fallen on people and killed them. No, you cannot make a connection between past sin and present suffering as the explanation.

Well then, you may wonder if there is some sort of a curse or evil influence hovering over me that scourges me and brings unbearable suffering. Jesus spent so much of his time freeing people from evil. I remember at the height of a suicide epidemic in North and West Belfast when in seven weeks fourteen young boys and girls took their own lives by suicide. The Wake is still a big event following all deaths, but especially suicide. Here for the first time young people see a 'mate', a friend laid out dead. The bewilderment is almost palpable and is certainly written all over their faces. They ask, 'Are we cursed?', 'Is God angry with us and punishing us?' The parents of the young dead simply ask, 'Why?'

It is at moments like these that I would love to have an answer to the mystery of suffering. I would love to be able to say something that would reduce the hurt, bathe the wounds and make the person feel better. But, there are no easy answers or sticking plasters that will take away the pain. Some in desperation go to fortune tellers for answers and comfort. Like the Rabbi in the story at the beginning, there is no simple explanation to the mystery of suffering. After all, Jesus did not heal everyone he met who was suffering.

But there is hope and we do have some indicators of what Jesus asks of us when we or a loved one face suffering that threatens to break us. Suffering contains its own seeds of hope. Some of the most wonderful miracles I have witnessed are carried out by 'ordinary' people when confronted with a suffering person. When I lived in America in mid-1980, the cook in the presbytery where I lived announced one day that he had been diagnosed as HIV positive. AIDS was still hardly known but soon would pass into the language of all cultures. Fred was his name and he went about for a few days utterly distraught and lost. None of the five of us priests living there knew what to do or even what to say. A lady called Carolyn, a grandmother, who came in daily to clean the house, succeeded in relating to Fred as nobody else could. I asked her how this had come about. Her reply was breathtaking in its simplicity, 'Fred, how can I help you now that you face this crisis?' 'Hold me and hug me' was his reply. He had become the leper of the twentieth century and Carolyn was not afraid to touch him. I never forgot that lesson. Suffering may scare us but not as much as it does the suffering person. Their hope is in your healing touch.

My temptation is to run away from suffering. But please don't run away from suffering. Charles of Mount Argus spent every day and many a night facing the reality of suffering. He never denied it or cloaked it. Following his example, we are called to grapple with suffering and not be afraid. Somewhere in the suffering is a trace of Jesus. I know that sounds strange, but there is a direct relationship between the Calvary Cross and your and my cross of suffering. They are made of the same stuff and while the nails, thorns, lance, spittle, mockery may be different, the feelings of isolation, being lost, even cheated and being afraid are just the same. There was no protective barrier around Jesus any more than there is around us.

Jesus was not ashamed about the death of his friend Lazarus. He shed tears of loss and went to the tomb of his friend. In Gethsemane Jesus not only shed tears but blood. He did not run away. On the Cross Jesus carried out a canonisation – this day you will be with me in Paradise – and absolved sins. He is the exemplar for all who suffer. Jesus showed that in suffering are the seeds of eternal life. A little girl and her dad were killed in a horrific car accident. Asked was she angry with God, the devastated mother of the child and wife replied 'No! God only takes the best and they were simply the best!'

Faith gives us a glimpse of the way forward. Calvary, yours and that of Jesus, always leads to Resurrection. Life is stronger than death. Good will eventually overcome evil. In all his blessing and care of the sick and suffering, Saint Charles was driven by faith. Hope was a constant theme of his life. He must at times have been overwhelmed by innocent suffering. On the other hand he was aware of sin and evil that seemed to go without any visible punishment or suffering. Charles never let his hope in God become diminished.

It is not easy to keep going in the face of suffering. Between Christmas Eve and 6 January 2005 I buried five babies from Holy Cross Parish in Belfast. At the graves I felt like kissing the ground because, as I looked at the parents in each situation, I knew we were standing on holy ground. They could not have kept going without God being powerfully present in them and with them. In some instances, they went back home to comfort and go on celebrating Christmas for their other children. Truly the Cross stands as a symbol of hope and victory.

Pope Benedict XVI holds up Mary, Mother of God on Calvary, as a model and inspiration:

> *Holy Mary, Mother of God,*
> *you have given the world its true light,*
> *Jesus, your Son – the Son of God.*
> *You abandoned yourself completely to God's call*
> *and thus became a well-spring of the*
> *goodness that flows from Him.*
> *Show us Jesus. Lead us to Him.*
> *Teach us to know and love Him,*
> *so that we can become capable of true love*
> *and be fountains of living water*
> *in the midst of a thirsty world. Amen.*

V

Doing God's Will

BRIAN D'ARCY CP

When I was asked to preach at the thanksgiving novena in Mount Argus. I felt I had to do something special.

But when I sat down to write a sermon about Father Charles, I found I had absolutely nothing new to say. It was then I accidentally saw an advertisement for cheap flights to Amsterdam. And I recognised instantly that 'Charlie' was guiding me. I did something I never do. I booked a flight with an overnight stay in Amsterdam. A nurse in Enniskillen, who has great devotion to Blessed Charles, had a friend in Holland. She got the instructions. I went to Amsterdam airport, caught a train and three hours later ended up in Sittard, the nearest large town to his birthplace.

There, a taxi driver took me to Munstergeleen and that is how I got to the wee country place Father Charles came from. There I discovered his house and the little church, a delightful oasis of peace. It was heavenly. And I knew that I would get the inspiration to tell, not what

I wanted to say, but what Father Charles wanted people to hear.

I sat and prayed most of the morning. I talked to everybody who came in and there were many, most them on bicycles. He is not forgotten.

I met the local priest and he was most welcoming. He was the priest responsible for pushing the miracle now accepted for the canonisation of Father Charles. He knew Dolf Dormans, the cured man, from seeing him at morning Mass and was the one who blessed him with a relic of Saint Charles. He brought me to the cured man's house.

It struck me how fitting it was that I should visit the home of Saint Charles and discover how, step-by-step, God led him from an obscure village to heaven, via Ireland.

I'm sure many a day Father Charles, walking the corridors of Mount Argus, yearned to do what I did – go back and spend a morning in the little peaceful village where he grew up. But he gave his life to God and accepted the consequences.

The Passionists, an Italian order, came to Ireland over a hundred and fifty years ago. We arrived in Mount Argus on 15 August 1856. Our most famous member was that Dutchman Father Charles Houben. He is a perfect example of God writing straight on crooked lines. Traditionally Passionists are supposed to conduct missions and retreats and, through our preaching, spread devotion to the Passion of Christ. Too often our preaching may have emphasised that it was our sins which caused Christ's suffering. That meant scrupulous people were left with a crippling sense of guilt. It is more encouraging and accurate to see Christ's Passion as the ultimate proof of God's love for us. That's what Father Charles always got right.

Father Charles was born in the quiet village of Mun-stergeleen and his life could be seen as a series of failures. He was a slow learner in his youth, one of eleven children in a poor family. It was only after his mother died that he could think about entering the priesthood. First, though, he was conscripted into the army and he was a failure there, too. But out of that failure he discovered a Passionist monastery and felt the call to become a Passionist. And he did. Before his ordination, however, his father died. The family were so poor they couldn't afford to go to his ordination, because of the expense of the funeral. Even happy days were lonely days. After ordination he was sent to England to help establish the Passionists there.

The priest whom the Passionists sent to found Mount Argus was a member of the English aristocracy, Lord Longford's great-uncle, Paul Mary Pakenham. He was a young man in his early thirties, a former officer in the British Army, highly intellectual and competent. A born leader, he was the ideal man to be the first rector of Mount Argus. However six months after he came to Ireland, he died unexpectedly. God's ways are not our ways.

They had no one else to send in his place except this Dutchman who knew little English and was so pedantic they couldn't allow him say a public Mass. He never conducted a mission and his only suitable tasks were blessing the sick and hearing confessions. Yet Mount Argus monastery was built on the reputation of this apparent failure, while the one the Passionists considered the ideal man was taken by God.

Despite his failures, Father Charles had something

people identified with and they came in their thousands to him for healing.

Every day, up to 300 people came to Mount Argus. It didn't impress his community in Mount Argus, many of whom didn't understand him. He became so popular with the people that the diocesan authorities, not to mention the medical profession, grew suspicious of him. They got their opening when a couple of Dublin rogues came to Father Charles and asked him to bless a barrel of holy water for them. They then sold it at a shilling a bottle as being 'blessed by the holy man of Mount Argus'. It's hard to beat the Dubs.

Poor Father Charles was banished to England and the best known priest in Ireland at the time had no one to see him off on the boat, except his trusted friend Brother Michael. Before he left, there were elaborate plans to build a new church and retreat house at Mount Argus. The foundation stone was laid before Charles was sent away, but during his eight years away Mount Argus went downhill and nearly closed.

Eventually it was decided to bring him back to Dublin. When he came back, Mount Argus took off. Once more people returned and Charles took up his healing ministry again. Mount Argus once more became so popular that they decided to resume building the church. The problem was nobody could remember where the foundation stone was laid, it was so overgrown. Nevertheless, because of Father Charles' ministry, Mount Argus was saved and the buildings we know today were completed. God allows us to make mistakes but when our foolishness has had its say, God will have his too.

When I entered the Passionists I had never heard of

Father Charles of Mount Argus. But as a student I soon understood his appeal. Compassion for the sick and dying were the hallmarks of his life.

In time I got to know the real Father Charles from Mrs Cranny. Her father brought him in a pony and trap to bless the sick around Dublin in the latter part of the nineteenth century. She herself was blessed and cured by him when she was a child. It was an effective blessing because she lived to be 107.

She remembered him clearly and insisted Father Charles wasn't a severe old man, with dead eyes looking down at the ground as he is often portrayed. On the contrary he was a smiling, friendly man and good fun. When her father brought him around Dublin to heal the sick, Charles always encouraged people to trust God to walk with them in their suffering, whether they were cured or not. We don't have to have answers to the problem of suffering but we should trust God not to abandon us.

For Charles, God isn't the cause of suffering but neither is suffering a curse. If we accept God's will, strength will come. He preached the Passion by telling simple stories about Christ's suffering and by reassuring the sick that their pain was linked to Christ's, and therefore never wasted. Mrs Cranny's father memorised his stories and repeated them to the family when he came home.

Unusually for a healer, Charles sometimes told those who came for a blessing that they wouldn't get better. There is a documented case where he said to a sick man, 'It is not God's will that you should get better, this is God's gift to you so that you should go home and prepare for your death'. The man to his credit accepted his advice and died a month later.

I experienced Charles's unusual way of answering prayers in my own life when as a young student my mother got sick. We prayed to Father Charles for guidance and healing, but Mammy died despite all our prayers.

I was devastated that my prayers weren't answered then; later in life, I realised that all prayers are answered, but not necessarily in the way we want. As the song says: 'Some of God's greatest gifts are unanswered prayers'. If my mother hadn't died, I am not sure I would have been a priest and I certainly would not be the kind of priest that I am.

My father worked on the railway but in 1962 he was told the railway was closing and he'd have to change to be a bus conductor. A short time afterwards, conductors were done away with and he had to learn to drive a bus. My father was over fifty years of age without a job and he asked me to send him a relic of Father Charles. He trained as a bus driver even though the only thing he had ever driven before that was a tractor, He passed the test and for the rest of his working life drove safely. But he'd never leave home without the plastic covered relic of Father Charles in his coat pocket, which was his way of showing his appreciation of Charles' intervention.

When I was Rector and parish priest of Mount Argus from 1983 to 1989, my biggest problem was the restoration of the monastery and church. In 1983 we discovered that the timbers and walls of the monastery and church were in an advanced state of dry rot. We had to take every slate off the roof, every rafter, every inch of plaster off the walls of both buildings. We had to lift all the floors in the monastery and restore the complete fabric from foundation to roof.

At first we thought about demolishing it, but because it was such an historic building, that was not possible and anyway the most economical solution by far was to restore it. It was a mammoth task.

But the reason it survived at all was Father Charles.

It's difficult for somebody who wasn't there to understand what an impossible task it was at the time. There were over eighty priests, brothers and students in the community.

In the 1980s Ireland was an economic mess. Unemployment was high; the best of our young, educated people emigrated to find work and a future. A Government Minister actually said that the island was too small for the number of people living on it and that it was a good experience for our talented graduates to emigrate. It was the worst possible time to ask people for money to restore a church and monastery.

Father Charles was the man I put my trust in. I lived in a small room next to the room where he died. I discovered then what a friend I had in Father Charles. I had to raise two and a half million pounds to save the buildings. To me it was a miracle it was ever completed and Charles was the miracle man.

By 1987, goodwill towards Mount Argus was exhausted. We had been going for over four years and we simply succumbed to charity fatigue.

We ran one last draw, the fifth in all. Three thousand participants paid one hundred punts each into what was supposed to be a massive draw. It turned out to be a disaster. The committee was afraid to tell me how bad it was. The leader, Joe Morris, called me into the office one morning and told me we were going to lose thousands.

I had always said that if Father Charles wanted Mount Argus to be restored, it would happen. All we had to do was the same as he had done: trust in God. But I was in no humour for pious thoughts that morning and in an off-handed way I said to Joe: 'Wouldn't you think, if Charlie wanted Mount Argus restored, he would get off his backside and help us'.

Poor Joe was shocked at my disrespectful attitude to such a saintly figure.

I went on to RTE to do an interview with Mike Murphy, but when I came back two hours later I was told that Rome had phoned in my absence to inform us that Father Charles would be beatified in a few months. That was his way of telling me that he was still in charge.

Needless to say the draw was filled, the Church was completed and we were even able to build a shrine to Blessed Charles as well.

Father Charles had three simple rules about suffering. He told the sick to thank God in the midst of their suffering, to offer their suffering up to God and to expect God's help and sometimes healing.

The great Dutch painter Vincent Van Gogh has a magnificent painting of an open Bible with a novel lying beside the Bible. The novel in question was a popular one at the time which his father, a minister, had banned him from reading. Van Gogh thought it was an excellent novel which chronicled family tragedies and family scandals. If you look closely you will see the Bible is open at Isaiah 53. It says: 'He took up our infirmities and carried our sorrows'. That was Van Gogh's way of linking the tragedies of daily life to God's journey with us.

Father Charles believed that Jesus walks with us during our suffering. It is a way of the cross. On the way of the cross Jesus fell three times but got up each time. He needed help. He needed Simon. He needed people. He needed a mother to touch him. He needed a towel from Veronica. He needed compassion from the women of Jerusalem. After his Resurrection he proudly displayed his wounds to Thomas.

Thomas is often referred to as 'Doubting Thomas' as if doubting was a sin. Doubt is not the opposite of faith; certainty is. Thomas wanted to see the wounds of Jesus. And when he did, he believed totally: 'My Lord and my God', he said, before going on to give his life to spreading the Gospel. Because of Thomas' doubts, we know for certain that Jesus carried the wounds of his Passion after his Resurrection, showing that the new life of the risen Jesus was won by the wounds he still bore. Saint Peter later summed it up by saying: 'By his wounds we are healed'. That's what Charles believed and furthermore he was convinced that our own woundedness, as well as the wounds of Jesus, saves us.

He knew that we don't need to be able to make sense of suffering, as long as we remember that 'Nothing is impossible with God'.

Charles is not a remote saint with nothing to offer our generation. As a Passionist, I should learn to look at his life and discover that our greatest gift is to be people of compassion; to be willing to walk with people along their way of the cross, in search of meaning rather than handing out futile answers.

Van Gogh also said that God always sends works of art so that we might recognise ourselves in the works of art. 'Christ is the greatest artist of all. He works not in canvas but with human flesh', he concluded. Saint Charles, for me, is a wonderful example of a human canvas that God made into a work of art. He was a poor preacher, ridiculed by those who lived with him. At the end of his life he suffered pain but remained human enough to have a sing-song and a glass of whiskey when he needed it. He's my kind of saint.

He called himself 'poor old Charlie' as he walked along the corridors. One lasting memory that Father Eugene Nevin (a contemporary in Mount Argus) had of Charles, was his fear of death as he hobbled down the fifty-nine steps from his cell on the top floor, to bless the sick in the parlours. All the while he repeated the second half of the Hail Mary: 'Holy Mary, Mother of God, pray for us sinners, now and at the hour of our death, Amen'.

In theory, Charles was not the ideal model of the perfect Passionist. Yet of all the Passionists who've lived and worked at Mount Argus for over 150 years, he's the only one to be canonised.

Through the bad times, Charles still keeps me going. There have been many times in the past, and I'm sure there will be many more in the future, when I wondered why I remained a priest or a Passionist. These days as I look back and reflect on my life honestly, there isn't much to enthuse over. But then I think of Charlie. An old man full of pain praying for a happy death, recognised by the people as a holy man but not really by those in his own house. And now he's a canonised saint in heaven. That's what keeps me going. Even broken failures like me can be a work of art when I allow God to work through me.

VI

The Passion-Pattern in Life

IGNATIUS WATERS CP

I tell you most solemnly, when you were young you put on your own belt and you walked where you liked but when you grow old, you will stretch out your hands and someone else will put a belt around you and lead you where you would rather not go.

John 21:18

Talking about time is a favourite subject of conversation when we are not talking about the weather or the neighbours. 'Where did the time go?', we ask, and we don't like the answer, especially when we are 'getting on'! Before I went away to Africa, I took my mother and a few nephews and nieces out to lunch. My mother ordered her favourite drink and the nephews and nieces ordered theirs and then disappeared. The waiter came to me and said, 'Excuse me, Sir, but we don't have that drink your wife ordered!' I got such a surprise that I stuttered, 'But she's not my wife; she's my mother!' The waiter got such a surprise that he never came back. He sent someone else instead. My mother was pleased but I wasn't!

We joke about it but we don't like it; we don't like to be 'getting on'. We don't like all the changes in ourselves, in our families; all the losses and separations that life brings. A South African writer wrote: 'The skin of his neck was beginning to sag. Why did an old person's skin stretch like a jersey that had been washed too often? When did the air start leaking from the balloon?' (*Entertaining Angels* by Marita Van Der Vyver.)

And yet we feel that we haven't even started yet: 'Wait till I get started!' We have achieved so little, we have so little to show, we seem to be going backwards instead of forward — and we don't like it!

Now, Jesus was human in every way that we are. So he, too, must have wondered where did the time go. Thirty-three years - that's all the time he had. He had every reason to believe he was only beginning and yet he knew he was coming to the end. And just like us, he felt he had little to show for all his efforts, he hadn't succeeded in the job he set out to do. And he didn't like it either! Jesus, you remember, warned Peter that he would be led in ways that he would rather not go. And he knew what he was talking about, because he himself had been led in ways he would rather not go — and he didn't have to wait till he was old! There were many agonies before the agony in the garden.

What does it mean to be human? There are many ways of describing it, but in the Scriptures being human, being flesh, means life apart from God, life separated from God. Because I am flesh, I will have needs, desires, centres of interest apart from God, that God can do nothing about unless he destroys me as a human being. As long as I am human, in this body, I'll need to eat, drink, and rest, no matter how spiritual I think I am or how much I pray. As long as I am human, in this body, with these hands, this brain, this heart, I will love my work, I will love my people, I will love my family, my friends. They will be centres of interest for me. They will occupy me (preoccupy me!); they will absorb my attention. I won't want to leave them — these people, these places! There is no way of avoiding this criss-cross of life unless God destroys us as human beings.

And Jesus, our human brother, had these same needs, these same desires, these same centres of interest.

He loved his work and, whether it was carpentry or teaching, he wanted to make a good job of it; he didn't want to leave a job undone or half done.

He loved his people, his mother, his friends and he didn't want to leave them; he didn't want to die.

> By his incarnation, the Son of God has united himself in some fashion with every person. He worked with human hands, he thought with a human mind, he acted by human choice, and he loved with a human heart.
>
> *Gaudium et Spes*, Article 22

His agony was the agony of a heart so deeply in love with people, yet feeling and knowing that they didn't understand him, that he wasn't getting through to them. Often, our greatest suffering can be that we are hurting people we love and don't want to hurt: people we love who are disappointed in us, who don't understand what we are trying to do, who are offended by what we are doing. I'll never forget the anguish (it could be called 'agony') of having to put my father into a nursing home because, in his senility, it was impossible to care for him at home. But he didn't understand that and it was just awful to see the pain, bewilderment and confusion in his eyes, and the accusing way he looked at us, 'You, that I trusted, are doing this to me!' After all the years, the memory is fresh with me still.

Jesus' pain was the agony of knowing that he was failing the very people he loved and wanted to help and disappointing them completely: 'We had hoped', they said. They trusted him and he was letting them down.

No wonder the temptation in the desert returns with force and buries his face in the dust — the temptation to save his people in some other way. No wonder he prays with 'loud cries and tears':

'Father, if it be possible ...

Father, it's hardly fair — Here I'm coming to the end before I've really started!

Father, please give me more time ... let me try again ...

Father I've failed miserably in the way you gave me to follow, the work you gave me to do.

Let me try again, let me try some other way ... the way the people wanted, the way my disciples wanted. Maybe if I haven't won them in your way I'll win them in that way!'

But always, he ends the prayer: 'But Father, not the way I want it (or the way the people want it) but the way you want it'. He yields, he surrenders, he allows himself to be led in ways he would rather not go. But not without a struggle!

This was the pattern of Jesus' life and it was the pattern of Charles' life. Charles, too, loved his people, his country, his own family. He communicated with them all over the years but after he left home and in the thirty years he lived here, he never saw them again! As you know, they weren't in Africa or in America but so close, we would think today, in the Netherlands. I'm sure Charles, like

Jesus, felt he had achieved so little after all the years. I'm sure he, too, felt a failure. He never succeeded in speaking English properly; he must have felt alone and lonely; some in the community thought he was a little touched, so 'wrought up in God', in the old phrase, that he walked into things and fell down manholes.

And, do you know he once had to be dried out? But not the way you're thinking! When his beatification was announced in 1988, his remains had to be exhumed for examination and even though his tomb was here in the church, water had seeped through and his poor bones were soaked, so for many weeks they lay on a tray in his room on the top floor – drying out! I used to slip in and look at them, this miserable pile of bones and skull and wonder, 'What's this old life all about?' Wondering, too, 'What's so special about these old bones?' I was still wondering through the pomp and glory of the beatification in Rome, seeing the tapestry of Charles unfurled and hanging in front of Saint Peter's, hearing the Pope speak of Dublin and Mount Argus and Charles, our Charles. It was marvellous and encouraging but I kept thinking of the pile of bones on the tray.

What made Charles different from all the other 'old bones' that lived here in one hundred and fifty years? Men who were far more gifted and intelligent, better teachers and preachers and leaders? The difference was that Charles was totally absorbed in God. Yes, he loved his people and his family but God was his all; he made his home in God. He truly was a man of God. And people instinctively, intuitively, recognised that. It didn't matter that he couldn't speak very well or preach very well. What he said came from the heart – and from a heart in tune with God. In simple words, Charles took God seriously as Jesus took God seriously and had no doubt that God was still at work in his life, even when everything seemed to be going wrong. Again, not without a struggle!

Maybe, at one time, we thought we were strong and perfect as a Church, as religious orders. The granite pile of Mount Argus was a symbol of our strength and we were proud of it. Now when we are smaller and older and more fragile, maybe God is trying to teach us that we were never strong, as a Church or as individuals. We are, and always were and always will be, more like a pitiful pile of dry bones. We are more like earthenware than granite, and that is reason for great hope. It's the triumph of failure. The more aware we are that we are earthenware, the more effective we can be because we deeply realise the treasure we carry comes from God and not from us, the power comes from God and not from us, the spirit comes from God and not from us.

VII

A Healing Blessing

FRANK KEEVINS CP

One morning, just after the Father Charles Novena Mass was over, I was called to the parlour having been told that there were some people looking to see a priest. When I got there I found a whole family waiting for me, and the focus of their concern was their little boy, Kevin, who at five years of age was going into hospital to have his fifth heart operation. The family wanted Kevin to be blessed with the relic of Saint Charles, which I duly did, and then I promised them that I would continue to pray for him throughout the Novena. It was a little while later that it occurred to me that this was how it all began, the journey to sainthood, with a sick little boy looking for a blessing.

The incident is recorded for us by Father Sebastian Keens, a member of the Passionist community at the time. He tells us that a boy of about twelve, having lost the use of his legs, was brought to Mount Argus by his mother to seek a blessing from a Passionist, not an uncommon request. Father Sebastian immediately summoned Father Charles to come and bless the boy, while he himself went

up to his room to change out of his habit and into his sec-
ular clothes, because he had to go into Dublin that day
and you couldn't wear the habit out in the streets. When
he came back downstairs, he was amazed to find the little
boy walking up and down in front of the house, perfectly
cured. From that day on, the word began to spread, other
reported cures followed, and people started coming to
Mount Argus not just to be blessed by a Passionist, but to
be blessed specifically by Father Charles. And no matter
how many people came or at what time of day, Father
Charles responded in his own humble, patient way. Day
after day of his life, he spent hour after hour imparting a
blessing on the sick and the weary and the broken.

The gospels show us that there is no other group of
people that Jesus had more time for than the sick, and
then later on the Church continued that ministry of
compassion, saying, 'If anyone is sick, bring them along
so that we may bless them as Jesus blessed them'. And,
of course, this is what inspired and motivated Father
Charles; he loved the sick as Jesus loved the sick, he had
time for the sick as Jesus had time for the sick, he blessed
the sick as Jesus blessed the sick, and this led people to
recognise that true holiness in him that came to fruition
in his canonisation.

Whenever we celebrate the Sacrament of Anointing,
we reflect once again that compassionate love of Jesus
for the sick, and that gentle blessing ministry of Father
Charles. We ask God to touch the lives of the sick as
they most need him to at this moment, and that will be
different, we know, for each one. It may be that God will
heal the sick of their infirmity; or that he will give them
grace to bear with pain. God may grant the strength to

resist the temptation to despair, to turn bitter, or to lose faith. God may grant a gift of prayer, or the generosity to offer one's sufferings for the healing of others. Or perhaps God will give the gift of drawing goodness out of others, and an appreciation of the health they have that the sick person doesn't have.

These are just some of the things the sick are called to be and to do in the Church, because whatever else they may lack for in their sickness, they are infinitely precious in God's eyes, and in Father Charles they have a saint who is praying for them and blessing them still. Those who are sick have a part to play in God's purposes that no one else can play. They can say 'Yes' to their sickness, and say 'Yes' to whatever way God will bless their life, knowing that God will take their 'Yes' and use it for the salvation of the world, since in the 'Yes' of each one of us, as in Mary's 'Yes', God says, 'Do not be afraid, I am with you, and I will give you all the graces that you need'.

VIII

The Stranger Among Us

MARTIN COFFEY CP

Saint Charles suffered quite a bit in his last few years. It is said that his friend Brother Michael asked him if he would like to go back to Holland to see his people. He replied, 'I can't go back. These are my people. I would be a stranger in Holland'. Charles no longer considered himself a stranger in his adopted homeland and certainly the people of Ireland considered him one of their own. At an early age Charles heard the call of Jesus to go out to the whole world and he responded with all his heart. He had the freedom to leave his own country and all he loved there because he shared God's love for the whole world, including a little island way off in the far west called Ireland. He believed that the Good News is for everyone. Nobody is excluded, no country is foreign. That is the great truth we celebrate here today. Christians are first and foremost citizens of the whole world, part of a new humanity established by Jesus, which includes every tribe and tongue and people and nation.

The stranger is a powerful figure in the Bible. Again and again God tells his people to welcome the stranger always, to provide him with food and shelter because they, the Israelites, were strangers, exiles in Egypt and they more than others know the hardships of the stranger's plight. This, God says, should make them sympathetic and compassionate towards the stranger who comes into their camp or is knocking on their door. The same could be said of the Irish. Generations of our forefathers and foremothers went as exiles, strangers, to every continent and settled there, many of them making their fortune and contributing significantly to the development of their new homelands. This fact of history teaches us the importance of hospitality.

Jesus also knew what it was to be a stranger. He humbled himself and suffered a kind of exile from his Father's house by choosing to live among us. He experienced welcome from Mary and Joseph who provided a home for him but a whole range of hostile and negative reactions from others who considered him, his teaching and behaviour very strange. His own received him not. They could not accept the word of a carpenter's son. He was dismissed as a 'nobody'. He knew from first hand experience what it was to be rejected, dismissed and accounted as nothing. He befriended the outcasts, the poor, the unclean, the heretics, the outsiders and foreigners because he identified with them. The gossip about him in the streets and alleyways, even among the educated and sophisticated, described him as a blasphemer, a drunkard, a friend of prostitutes and sinners. Jesus was the friend of strangers.

Jesus opens his heart in fellowship with the outcast and the stranger. That is why Jesus raised on the Cross draws all people to himself and establishes a new unity, a new equality, a new way of belonging together in the family of the Father. No one is excluded, no one is a stranger. This is the Kingdom of God. We take our lead from him. We live our Christian discipleship by reflecting his openness and kindness to the stranger who then becomes our friend. Jesus puts it up to us. He warns us that following him will not be easy. If you want to be my disciple then this is what it involves. We are to build a new humanity where old divisions based on colour, race and wealth are brushed aside, a new humanity from which racism, prejudice and bigotry have been banished.

From the very beginning, Christians were different. They were part of a revolutionary movement that broke with the religious conventions and beliefs of the time. The new Christian faith was regarded as a scandal by Jews and the Romans and Greeks thought it both crazy and dangerous. Christians were very strange indeed. They refused to identify with any particular people or place. They broke every taboo, crossed every boundary; they welcomed every kind of person into the community. Christians were the first to talk about the whole of humanity as one family under the one God who is Father of all. Saint Peter proclaimed in the house of the Gentile Cornelius, 'Now we see that God has no favourites but accepts men and women from every nation'. Saint Paul wrote that by his Cross Jesus tore down the walls separating people so that there is no longer Jew and non-Jew, Greeks and non-Greeks, slave and free because now all are one in Christ. God's plan is to unite all things in heaven and earth. This is also the mission of every Christian.

But the message is even more radical than that. We are not only one but equal as well. When Saint Paul was asked to reconcile the feuding factions in the City of Corinth, he insisted that they accept and forgive each other because, he said, 'this is your brother, this is your sister, this is the one for whom Christ died', 'your sister has been purchased by the precious blood of the Lamb'. In other words, your brother is of infinite value and is to be accepted, respected and loved as such. Christianity was a radically new and challenging kind of religion. All the old suspicions, enmities, divisions that keep people apart have been cancelled and abolished forever. As Saint Paul says, 'you must preserve the unity of the Spirit by the peace that binds you together.'

The Gospel message is truly revolutionary. The followers of Jesus have been transformed and given a new identity. Once again, Saint Paul says it best, 'look at me, it is no longer I who live, it is Christ who lives in me', 'my true life is hidden with Christ in God'. The new reality brought about by Jesus re-shapes us and re-directs us and gives us a whole new sense of what it means to be human.

Now Christ is our life so that from now on we see with his eyes and love with his heart. We are a new creation because Christ is living in us. And so whatever I do to you, I do to Christ. When I give you bread, I give bread to Christ; when I welcome you, I welcome Christ. If I reject you, if I refuse to welcome you, I am rejecting Christ, since it is no longer simply you that I meet, but Christ living in you. 'As long as you do it to the least of these you do it to me.'

We live in a dangerous world divided between them and us, or as some put it between the 'West and the Rest'. We find ourselves on one side of that divide because we are wealthy, successful, white Europeans. The Rest includes most of the East, the Arab world and the Middle East, Eastern Europe and Africa. The West sees itself as rich, successful and superior. The Rest pose a threat either because they reject what we believe and value or because they want a share of it. So for the sake of our security we either eliminate the threat by invading Iraq and threatening Iran, declaring war on unknown terrorists, or we defend ourselves by building barriers and borders and keeping them out. All the time the tension is rising and we grow in fear. Suspicion and hostility are increasing. In this climate we risk being carried along by the tide and so abandoning the revolutionary message of Jesus that we all belong together in the one family of God.

Perfect love casts out fear. We must choose between love and fear. Fear only activates all that is narrow and negative in our nature. It affects how we see the world and how we relate to people. It makes us suspicious, closed, self-protective and self-preoccupied. It makes us want to isolate ourselves or to dominate others. It leads inevitably to hatred and conflict. Fear makes us blind and stupid. In the end fear robs us of our humanity. It is fear that causes man's inhumanity to man.

Choose love, choose life. Jesus shows us the way of love and that's the model Saint Charles chose to follow. The Dutchman Charles Houben came to Ireland and made his home here. Like Saint Patrick before him, he was an exile, a foreigner, chosen by God to be an unexpected blessing to the Irish. He had a great impact on Dublin through his healing and kindness, especially to the poor, and the people responded with a huge outpouring of love and devotion that continues to this day. No other member of the Mount Argus community then or since has had anything like the same impact on the people and the city of Dublin.

Like all immigrants, he suffered as he struggled to make his place here among us. In the first place, he missed his homeland, his family and friends. He had great difficulties with the language and some say he never really mastered it. He suffered at the hands of his own brethren who considered him very strange; some even thought him insane. However, none of this prevented him from settling here and reaching out to people who opened their hearts to him and welcomed him into their homes and their lives. They weren't distracted by his heavy accent or inability to speak well. The ordinary people of Dublin saw him clearly and simply as a good and holy man. They experienced kindness, compassion and healing from him. He touched them with the warmth of his heart and they saw the love of Christ in his gentle eyes. His goodness and sanctity shone out undimmed by any considerations of a petty nature.

Like so many immigrants before him, Saint Charles became more Irish than the Irish themselves. Being a foreigner, a non-national, was no great disadvantage to him in his ministry.

Saint Charles was revered by everyone because of the kind of man he was. The people responded to him so warmly also because hospitality to the stranger was a strong feature of the faith of the Irish. Charles found himself among a people who still lived with the memory of persecution and famine. They knew what it was to be shunned and rejected, to be misunderstood, subject to suspicion and hostility. During centuries of persecution travellers, people on the run, the poor of the road were welcomed and given food and shelter. Whenever a stranger knocked on the door he was welcomed because he represented Christ who was himself refused lodgings, locked out and had nowhere to lay his head. The people of Dublin welcomed Charles because they knew that Christ still comes in the form of a stranger. That faith is beautifully expressed in this ancient poem translated from Irish:

> *Then when the shiuler comes*
> *Be neither hard nor cold*
> *The share that goes for Christ*
> *Comes back a hundred fold.*
>
> *If there be a guest in your house*
> *And you conceal aught from him*
> *'Tis not the guest that will be without*
> *But Jesus, Mary's Son.*

One awful reaction to the stranger in our midst is racism. Racism is the worst form of prejudice and it is very widespread in Europe and Ireland today. I worked for many years in Africa and met racism face to face. I knew a black priest in South Africa who was not accepted by the people in a white parish. He talked to them one day. 'If you do not like me because I am ignorant, I can be sent to school and educated. If you do not like me because I am dirty, I can be taught to wash and be clean. If you do not like me because of my unsocial habits, I can learn to live in your society. But if you do not like me because of the colour of my skin, I can only refer you to the God who made me.'

Racism, like every form of prejudice, thrives on rumours and half truths. It feeds irrational fears and anxieties. It builds up an insurmountable wall of misunderstanding and mistrust between people. It is the total negation of the Gospel and must be resisted in the name of Christ.

Just as countless Irish people went abroad to seek their fortune in harder times and contributed to the development of the United States, Australia and other places, so a new era of migration has started and Ireland is on the receiving end. We are the first generation of Irish people to be hosts to those who come to our shores full of dreams and hopes of a better life among us. They see Ireland as a place of fresh starts and new opportunities. Like our forefathers, many people are coming to our shores driven away from their own place by hardship and lack of opportunity. Our own history of hardship and suffering has prepared us to open the door of welcome.

Hospitality and welcome are indispensable as the global village becomes smaller and smaller. The arrival of so many people on our shores from as far away as Asia and Africa is not a curse but rather a blessing, offering us an opportunity to mature as a people and to exercise the Christian virtues of tolerance and hospitality like never before. The stranger need not be an enemy but a source of unexpected riches. The stranger is a friend in waiting, a fellow traveller with whom I can break bread.

Charles Houben is a famous immigrant who came to Ireland 150 years ago and enriched our country greatly. Ireland opened her arms to welcome him and so a stranger became a friend. Saint Charles should be declared the patron saint of immigrants. They can look to him for inspiration. They will find encouragement in his story when they feel lonely and isolated in a strange land. They can begin to hope that they too will be received with warmth and welcome when they see how the ordinary people of Dublin opened their hearts and their homes to this strange man from a foreign land over a century ago. Like Charles, they will be able to make their home here, find new friends, share their gifts and talents, become part of the community and contribute in a thousand different ways to the country. And we too can learn from the experience of Saint Charles that the stranger is often sent by God to bring unexpected and abundant blessings.

IX

A Mother's Love

MARTIN COFFEY CP

One thing we all have in common is that we are all our mothers' children. Sadly, a small number of people have never known their mothers, either because they were very young when their mothers died or because they have been adopted. But there is a mother figure in most of our lives, the one who nurtured and cared for us in the vital early years. She more than anyone else helped us adapt to this world and find our feet. Our mother is the one whose love and warmth can still be felt deep inside us, comforting and consoling us in the dark times.

Each one of us can say 'I am who I am because of my mother'. People who knew her say I am the image of my mother – I have her hair and her eyes but she wasn't 6'2". More than that, I have some of her temperament, her way of coping, her likes and dislikes. In other words, I am my mother's son. We remember our mothers with gratitude because we owe so much to them and we also thank Jesus for giving us his mother Mary to be a mother who inspires us to hope.

Blessed Charles had a special devotion to the Mother

of Hope because he set foot in Ireland for the first time on the feast of Mary, Mother of Hope in the year 1857. He had a copy of that lovely picture in his room that depicts the child Jesus in his mother's arms pointing to the Cross as if to say 'for this I came into the world'. It was the love and guidance of Mary that prepared Jesus for his mission and accompanied him from the poor stable of Bethlehem to the hill of Calvary.

Jesus was also the image of his mother. Formed in her womb, he borrowed his humanity from her, he was flesh of her flesh, bone of her bone. It was her blood that flowed in his veins. Those who looked at the little baby in his crib could see her features, her hair, the colour of her eyes, the shape of her nose. He was indeed his mother's son.

Jesus was the image of his mother also because of what he learned from Mary. She was his first teacher and guide. A woman of prayer, she pondered the Word of God deep in her heart, and taught the child Jesus how to pray. Her prayer became his prayer; 'be it done unto me according to thy Word' became his 'not my will but yours be done'. Mary was the embodiment of the Beatitudes. She was poor, meek and thirsting for what is right. Mary's sentiments nourished the young Jesus and one day he would leave her home and go with Good News to the poor just as his mother taught him. 'How blessed are you who are poor.'

When the angel appeared out of the blue, Mary didn't know how to respond or what to say. But eventually she said Yes, *fiat*, let it be. She had faith in God's word and hope for the future. She couldn't see how things were going to work out or what people would think. The risk of her Yes was great and initially everything did seem to go wrong. The misunderstanding of Joseph must have caused her great pain, the slaughter of the innocent children because of her child, her bewilderment at his mission, worrying that he might be harmed, wanting to protect him, seeing him mocked and brutally put to death.

Mary the woman of hope said Yes! I believe! I trust all will be well. Despite the great risk, there was an ease about her response to the angel that showed how much she was already in tune with God's ways and able to see that her happiness and fulfillment would follow from her Yes. She did not seek or expect privileges but was happy because deep down she was aware of the mysterious unfolding of God's plan for the world and her part in that. Yes, there would be hardship, but in the greater scheme of things the sufferings of her life were as nothing compared with the good that would be achieved for the world through her son, Jesus.

In Saint John's Gospel, Mary is at the heart of every gathering. Her first appearance is as a guest at the famous wedding of Cana. She is the one who gets the party going in earnest when she persuades her son to provide generous gallons of the best wine. It is highly significant that Jesus' first miracle is at a wedding. The marriage feast is a key symbol of the joy and festivity that Jesus has come to share with us. The Kingdom of God, he tells us, is like a great feast where there is an abundance of every good thing. Above all, the wedding feast is a gathering of friends and a celebration of love. And Mary is at the heart of it all. 'Look', she says, 'they have no wine for the party'. We see Mary in a new and charming light as a source of joy and laughter and fun for her friends and neighbours.

It is the same Mary that Jesus asks to be a mother to us and a source of inspiration and hope.

We marvel at her strong faith and hope and pray for some share in it. Faith is a many sided diamond. It includes the things we believe and recite in the Creed. But it is more than that. Faith invites us to dwell in a much bigger world that opens up new possibilities and that encourages great expectations. It brings us into a world where God is active and his Spirit is moving. Men and women of faith follow a way that appears increasingly strange to a modern world. There is a foolishness about people of faith. We live in a different atmosphere. We inhabit a different space, another kingdom. It is the Kingdom of God.

Our faith is nourished on wonderful stories that are full of mystery and magic: a story that begins with a virgin birth, angels singing in the night sky, shepherds and kings, and ends with the stone miraculously rolled back and men dressed in white declaring he is risen. The extravagance of this poetic language is the only way of capturing the wonder of God's ways and of pointing out the marvel of his blessings.

We live in dull times that are crying out for a restoration of magic. People complain of being tired and bored at our church services. There is a hunger for something more. The adventures of Star Wars, Harry Potter and The Lord of the Rings have captured the imagination of millions. Even the Da Vinci Code is a plea for magic and adventure in grey times. We Church people have contributed to the demise of the sense of wonder and the power of imagination by trying too hard to be ordinary when in fact by profession we claim to inhabit an extraordinary world where God dwells among his people. Part of our vocation is to witness to this other dimension and to keep alive the sense of wonder and magic. Too many people are sleepwalking through life on the way to the grave. We want people to be awake, alert, aware that the world is full of wonder because the world is full of God's wonderful presence. We want to awaken people to the wonder and mystery of it all.

Faith is shorthand for a whole way of life that flows from a new vision of reality. It is like having our eyes washed in the clear refreshing waters of a mountain stream. Now we see with new eyes. Everything glistens with a new freshness, everything appears in a brighter light. Things once familiar strike us as new, things never seen before are now luminously clear. We find ourselves in a world that is bursting with life and light and goodness. Nothing any more is ordinary or drab or dull.

The poets more than others have kept this dimension of faith alive for us. They help us to see the wonder and marvel of God's hidden presence in every little thing.

> *Earth is crammed with heaven*
> *And every common bush alive with God*
> *Only he who sees takes off his shoes*
> *The rest sit 'round and miss the magic.*

Mary's faith was expressed in the simple Joy of Being, 'my soul glorifies the Lord, my spirit exults in God my Saviour'. The life of faith is gratitude for every breath, for every beat of the heart, for every step we take. All our sitting, looking, hearing, every thought and feeling, every moment here and now is full to the brim with the energy of life – and for it all we say 'Thanks!' This is the fullness of life that Jesus offers. It is a new way of being in the world freed of all darkness and confusion, freed of conflict, suspicion and fear. The gift of faith is like an awakening, an immersion into a new dimension of being. It is marked by peaceful acceptance of reality as it is – of people and events, of the past, the present, the future. No crippling regrets about the past, no paralysing anxiety about the future. It is total presence in the here and now. It is a life free of all craving and grasping; with no need to control or dominate; without judgement or criticism, without hostility or attachment. It is a total peaceful and joyful presence in the here and now and a marvelling at it all.

Jesus said the Kingdom of God is very near to us. It is right before our eyes. Happy are those who have eyes to see! It shines through every little thing. This is the presence of God, this is the Kingdom here and now. Faith is putting on the mind of Christ, seeing with his eyes, responding with his compassion, being in the world in a fuller and more peaceful way.

Mary was able to stay at Jesus' side right to the end because she was full of courage and confidence. At first there was a moment of hesitation, 'how can this be?', but in the end she leans on God, relies on him and trusts in his word. She couldn't have done it without a basic sense of personal well-being. This is another essential dimension of faith. Mary knew that when God created her he took the clay of the earth, breathed into it and filled her with life, the very breath of God. And God saw her and said, You are very good. Mary knew in her deepest being that every time God looked at her, he smiled and said 'you are great, you are wonderful, you are very good indeed'.

That is exactly what God says to you and to me. From the moment he formed you and breathed life into you, he saw you and said, 'You are great, you are beautiful because you are my image and likeness'. And he has never changed his mind and will never change his mind, and to this day every time God looks at you he says, 'Yes! You are great.' Nothing will change God's mind, nothing can take that away, nothing can rob us of our basic fundamental goodness. Nothing can erase the image of God stamped on our being.

Faith leads to this total acceptance ... I am — You are — It is. How wonderful, how great everything is! The Good News is 'You are somebody, not nobody.' You are who you are because that's the way God created you, and that's the way God wants you to be. That's the way God loves you. You have been given everything you need to be the very best kind of person possible. You really have all the gifts and talents, all the potential necessary for a full and fulfilled life. There is nothing outside you, no person or thing, no success or achievement that you need to make you a better person. You can become the full beautiful person God created you to be by discovering and accepting with gratitude who you are with all your gifts and by sharing that willingly with others. That, I believe, is the secret of a truly happy life.

And that is the Good News. Don't listen to the many versions of the Bad News, don't listen to those voices inside and outside that say how bad, how awful, how wretched you are. It isn't true! The deepest truth about us is that fundamentally we are truly blessed and good.

All we need has already been given to us by God. The seeds of joy, peace, happiness have been sown in the garden of our being. All we have to do now is to water those seeds and help them to grow.

Mary is there at the end too. 'By the Cross of Jesus stood his mother.' Mary is on Calvary keeping watch with her dying son. A silent, wordless presence supporting him with her love and understanding. Once again she utters her unbelievable prayer of trust 'Let it be done'. She longed to take him into her arms, to heal his wounds and quench his thirst but she could not. Her presence near her son, though silent and still, was a real sharing in the suffering of Jesus. Her attitude of faithful presence spoke of love and compassion, and however lonely and broken Jesus felt, the presence of his mother surely lightened the burden and brought him some comfort. Despite the insults and mockery, her presence assured him of his dignity as one loved and cherished.

Today we remember Mary as the Mother of Hope who was there when all appeared to be lost. Mary stands at the foot of the Cross and watches helplessly as her son dies in agony. Everyone has run away but Mary is constant. In the darkness of that Friday the fire of love continues to burn in her heart, the light of hope shines in her eyes.

When Jesus speaks those last words to his mother from the Cross, 'Woman this is your son', he is not thinking of himself, or looking for comfort and sympathy. He is already preparing the future. Mary is to go with John and become the heart of the new community. It will be a community of love and friendship nourished on the memory of Jesus who gave himself so completely on the Cross for love of us. Mary is the Mother of Hope because she is the mother of the new age that starts with Calvary, and the mother of the new community, the Church, that has its roots in the love of Jesus who died on the Cross for us. From the Cross, Jesus entrusts the future to Mary, Mother of Hope.

Mary the Mother of Hope was an inspiration to Saint Charles as she was also to Saint Paul of the Cross before that. Paul of the Cross was inspired to found the Passionists by Mary who appeared to him dressed in the distinctive black habit of the Passion. She wanted him to gather companions who would stand with her at the foot of the Cross and be with Jesus in his time of suffering and be with all who suffer, especially the victims of cruelty and injustice, the lonely and rejected. Compassionate presence was often the vocation of Mary as she watched her son from a distance making his way through the towns and villages and on to Jerusalem. He knew that he was never alone, didn't suffer alone, and as he breathed his last his mother was there by his side.

Saint Charles of Mount Argus was a Passionist. That was his inspiration and motivation in doing all he did for the poor and the suffering of Dublin. Like all Passionists, he stood with Mary at the foot of the Cross and had his gaze firmly fixed on Jesus giving his life in love for us. Everything he knew about love and kindness and the service of others he learned there. He travelled the streets of Dublin visiting the poor and sick in their homes and in hospitals bringing comfort and healing. Like Jesus he attracted crowds who wanted to see, hear and touch him.

All the time Charles was simply living his Passionist vocation of gazing on Jesus and learning from him. If he were here now, Charles would tell us to look beyond him to the Cross and see Jesus who emptied himself and freely chose to enter our world with all its variety but especially its suffering, sin, poverty. Jesus chose to live among the most needy people; he sought out and cared for the rejected and neglected. These were the people he fed with an abundance of bread. He healed their sufferings and forgave their sins. He threw his arms around them and assured them that they were all right. He countered the hostility and rejection that broke so many hearts and lives. That is still where Jesus chooses to be. He is one with the poor and the suffering, the lonely and the rejected. That's where the Passionist needs to be, together with Mary standing at the foot of the Cross comforting the afflicted of the world. Saint Charles was certainly there.

Saint Charles watered the seeds of joy and peace in the hearts of many people and continues to do so today. He had the eyes of faith to see the goodness in every human being. He was alive to the beauty and wonder of God's goodness everywhere. His canonisation is the recognition of all the ways he communicated God's great love and acceptance of people.

Ironically Charles would be the very last person to want such attention. Every picture shows the pained expression of an extremely shy retiring man thrust into the limelight. For him, canonisation is no doubt an opportunity to remind us of what is really important in life – namely to seek and find God: to know that we are loved, to experience a new peace in self-acceptance, to put our many talents and gifts to good use in the service of others. This simple, humble, very ordinary man became great because he gave all he had generously. He had faith and he led people to God; he had love and he showed compassion to the suffering; he had hope and he helped people to see beyond the troubles of the moment. If he were here now I think he would say, 'Don't look at me, look beyond. See the good and loving God, fix your gaze on him and be filled with his love and his peace. Do whatever he tells you'.

To Heal the Broken Hearted

The Life of Saint Charles of Mount Argus

Paul Francis Spencer CP

ISBN 978-1-905965-02-1

For almost thirty years Saint Charles, who died in 1893, was visited daily by hundreds of people who came to Mount Argus in Dublin to receive his blessing and to be prayed over for physical, emotional and spiritual healing.

Remembered by those who knew him as being 'always accessible', ready to go at a moment's notice to visit the sick and the dying, Saint Charles Houben was known throughout Ireland as the 'Saint of Mount Argus'. Yet he was no plaster saint, untouched by human weakness.

This biography reveals Charles' own inner struggles through which he learned compassion and understanding for others. Removed from Dublin for a time 'because of his extraordinary cures', he was until the end of his life subjected to criticism and humiliation, even within his own religious community. Crippled by constant pain in his later years, he continued to devote his life to the poor, the sick and the needy. Drawing the strength to bear his own suffering from the Passion of Christ, he was able to bring to them the compassionate love of Jesus Crucified.

We see Charles as someone who even in the midst of activity was able to live continually in the presence of God. His life exemplifies that fusion of action and contemplation which was intrinsic to his vocation as a Passionist. Following the teaching of Saint Paul of the Cross, the founder of the Passionists, Charles centered all his prayer and activity on the Mystery of the Cross. His life manifests his deep awareness of the profound link between the Crucified Christ and the crucified ones of our world.

Paul Francis Spencer CP, edited *Letters of Father Charles* (Passionist Publications, 1985) and translated with Martin Coffey CP *In the Heart of God: The Spiritual Teaching of Saint Paul of the Cross* (Passionist Publications, 1985). In 1994 his work *As a Seal Upon Your Heart: The Life of Saint Paul of the Cross, Founder of the Passionists* was published with St Pauls.

Available from Mungo Books

Mungo Books is an imprint of Ovada Books devoted
to publications of Scottish Catholic interest.

A Cairn of Small Stones

John Watts

ISBN 1–905965–001

This is a tale of the West Highlands in the eighteenth century,
told as the autobiography of a tenant farmer of North Morar. As
Ian More McLellan recounts his life story we are carried through
ninety dramatic years — through the risings of 1715 and 1745 and
their aftermath, the famines of the '70s and '80s, the emigrations
to the New World and the breaking up of the old clan society.
These form the backdrop to his own daily family life as son, hus-
band, father and grandfather, and as a farmer who also turned his
hand to droving, lead mining and sea-fishing.

An exceedingly well framed novel … [with] immense feeling for
the land and its people. A scholarly work, but written by a man
too informed to be patronising, too compassionate not to leave
his reader with a sense of magic of the glen and the strength of its
people.

— *The Catholic Times*

John Watts is the author of several works of history, including: *Scalan: The Forbid-
den College 1716–1799* (1999), *Hugh MacDonald: Highlander, Jacobite & Bishop* (2002)
and *A Canticle of Love: The Story of the Franciscan Sisters of the Immaculate Conception*
(2006).

Eilein na h-Òige: The Poems of Father Allan McDonald
edited by **Ronald Black**
ISBN 1-901157-61-X

The name of Father Allan McDonald (*Maighstir Ailein*), 1859–1905, is evergreen in the Gaelic-speaking islands of Uist, Barra and Eriskay. A native of Fort William, he wore himself out in the service of his parishoners at Daliburgh, and was transferred in 1894 to Eriskay, his beloved *Eilein na h-Òige* ('Isle of Youth'). Among his labours was the publication of a Gaelic hymnal which Ronald Black, the editor, has combined selections of in this volume with 27 poems first published in 1965, providing a resulting body of some 60 items with an English translation, introduction and notes.

A priceless treasure
— *Flourish*

A very valuable mine of information on Father Allan and Catholic Gaeldom
— Abbot Mark Dilworth

Ronald Black is Gaelic editor of *The Scotsman* and the Uist newspaper *Am Pàipear*. He has published *An Tuil: Anthology of 20th Century Scottish Gaelic Verse* (1999), *Smuaintean fo Éiseabhal* (2000) the poetry of Dòmhnall Aonghais Bhàin of South Uist, and *An Lasair: Anthology of 18th Century Scottish Gaelic Verse* (2001).

Ovada Books, an activity of the Passionists in Scotland and Ireland, has as its aims the promotion of Catholic faith and culture; supporting the ministry of the Passionists; and helping people to understand the Catholic Faith through publishing retailing and other means.

If you would like further information on how you can help our work, please contact us at

Ovada Books
Saint Mungo's Retreat
52 Parson Street
Glasgow
G4 0RX

Tel/Fax +44 (0)141 552 5523

Scottish Charity Number SCO 15760
The Passionists

xxi v
Ann.Dō
Set in mmvii
MT Spectrum
xii × xiv.iv × xxi,
by Monotype,
based on
Jan van Krimpen
designs of 1941–1943